KITCHEN KITSCH

VINTAGE FOOD GRAPHICS

Ed. Jim Heimann

TASCHEN

KÖLN LONDON MADRID NEW YORK PARIS TOKYO

Kitchen Kitsch

The lady of the house was the object of much attention by American advertisers for almost all of the twentieth century. Sequestered at home, her typical domestic duties included child rearing, cleaning, ironing, shopping and, above all, providing meals for all members of the household. The kitchen was her domain and it was here that Aunt Jemima®, Jell-O®, Weber® and Velveeta® courted her attention and brand loyalty.

From the very start of the century, food companies recognized the value of providing homemakers with free booklets espousing products and providing recipes for using them. So successful were these premiums that they became fixtures in every housewife's kitchen as food companies produced them *en masse*. Almost every American company offering items that would find their way into the kitchen produced a booklet of some sort. Sardines, dates, flour, cheese, beef, whipped cream, rice, potatoes – you name it and there was a pamphlet extolling its virtues.

Subsidiary industries also joined the bandwagon promoting broader agendas. Meat institutes, dairy farmers, egg producers, citrus co-ops and the avocado board might also release booklets praising their respective products and how to prepare them, giving them away at county fairs or at the local grocery store. Joining the food industry were the various appliance companies who might include recipe booklets along with their blenders, stoves or barbecues. Canning companies, skillet manufacturers and others also found this a unique opportunity to demonstrate the indispensability of their products.

By far the most common means of distribution was through the mail. An advertisement placed in a women's magazine became the initial contact. By sending in the coupon, the lucky homemaker would find a booklet rushed to her mailbox. Recipe booklets could also be included in the packaging or attached to the product itself.

The illustrations contained in many of the booklets were especially fine examples of their oeuvre and a primary factor in their appeal to collectors. While most were the product of anonymous commercial artists and illustrators, there were some exceptions, such as several done for Jell-O® by Maxfield Parrish. The period prior to mid-century was particularly rich in showcasing a commercial artist's ability to portray the food and products in a highly stylized manner. Produced by masters of color and composition, these illustrations romanced their audience with tantalizing visions of the culinary art. Often the artistic interpretations were hard to duplicate in the kitchen, but the visual appeal was the great seducer. Early attempts at food photography were less successful, but eventually, as technology improved, it became the dominant medium for most of the brochures after the 1950s.

As less time was spent in the kitchen and the traditional dinner hour was supplanted by fast food meals, the slow demise of the free recipe booklets took hold. Advertising through magazines also decreased as advertisers shifted their budgets to television. Added to these factors was the additional cost of producing the pamphlets for free distribution with little return for the advertising dollar. Eventually these realities contributed to the demise of this bit of Americana. Their void has created yet another category of the antiquated arts to be logged in the American memory bank and a fertile new field for collectors to pursue. Meanwhile, they provide an intriguing insight to American eating habits in the twentieth century and a gentle reminder of simpler times.

Küchenkitsch

Die Hausfrau gehörte im 20. Jahrhundert fast immer zur Zielgruppe der amerikanischen Werbung. Allein im eigenen Heim widmete sie sich den typisch häuslichen Pflichten wie der Kindererziehung, dem Putzen und Einkaufen und natürlich der Verpflegung aller Haushaltsmitglieder. Die Küche war ihr Terrain und hier bemühten sich Marken wie Aunt Jemima®, Jell-O®, Weber® und Velveeta® um ihre Aufmerksamkeit und Markentreue.

Schon zu Beginn des 20. Jahrhunderts hatten Lebensmittelhersteller erkannt, welches Potenzial in kostenlosen Werbemitteln lag, die der Hausfrau die Produkte vorstellten und ihr gleichzeitig Rezepte für deren Verwendung lieferten. Diese Broschüren wurden so erfolgreich, dass sie sich zur Standardausrüstung jeder Küche entwickelten und von den Unternehmen *en masse* produziert wurden. Fast jedes amerikanische Unternehmen, das Essbares in seinem Sortiment hatte, produzierte bald solche Broschüren. Ob es sich um Sardinen oder Datteln, Mehl, Käse, Rindfleisch oder Schlagsahne, Reis oder auch Kartoffeln handelte – bald hatte jedes erdenkliche Produkt seinen eigenen Prospekt vorzuweisen, der seine Vorzüge pries.

Tochterunternehmen schlossen sich diesem Trend an, um mehr Werbung für eine breitere Produktpalette zu machen. Interessenverbände wie die der Fleischindustrie, Molkereien, Eierlieferanten, Avocadozüchter oder Zitrus-Kooperativen gaben ihrerseits Broschüren heraus, die auf Messen verteilt wurden oder im Lebensmittelgeschäft um die Ecke auslagen. Auch sie priesen ihre jeweiligen Produkte an und enthielten zudem Hinweise für deren Zubereitung. Als Nächstes stieß die Haushaltsgeräteindustrie hinzu und warb mit Rezepten und Anwendungstipps für ihre Mixer, Herde, Pfannen und Grills. Letztlich erkannte auch die Konservenindustrie die einzigartige Möglichkeit, ihre Produkte als unverzichtbar darzustellen.

Die Abbildungen in vielen dieser Broschüren waren sehr kunstvolle Beispiele für ihr Genre und stellten damit einen großen Anreiz für Sammler dar. Größtenteils stammten die Arbeiten aus der Feder namenloser Grafiker und Illustratoren, doch auch bekannte Künstler wie Maxfield Parrish waren vertreten, der mehrere Arbeiten für Jell-O® lieferte. Bis zur Jahrhundertmitte stellten die Illustrationen das Geschick des Grafikers unter Beweis, die unterschiedlichen Lebensmittel und Waren in sehr stilisierter Form darzustellen. Die Industrie suchte sich dazu Könner in Sachen Farbe und Bildgestaltung, die ihre Leserschaft mit verlockenden Visionen wahrer Küchenkunst verführen sollten. Meist waren diese künstlerischen Interpretationen in der heimischen Küche kaum umzusetzen, aber gerade die visuelle Perfektion machte den Reiz der Abbildungen aus. Frühe Versuche im Bereich der Foodfotografie waren weniger erfolgreich. Erst mit der verbesserten Technik der 50er Jahre wurde die Fotografie im Großteil dieser Broschüren zum vorherrschenden Medium.

Je weniger Zeit in der Küche verbracht und je mehr das traditionelle gemeinsame Abendessen von Fast Food verdrängt wurde, desto stärker wurden diese Prospekte vom Markt gedrängt. Auch das Werbeverhalten wandelte sich: Es wurde immer weniger in Zeitschriftenanzeigen und immer mehr in Fernsehwerbung investiert. Ein weiterer Faktor für den Rückgang waren die Kosten für die Produktion der Broschüren, die immer weniger Rendite einbrachten. Letztendlich waren es diese veränderten Umstände, die den Niedergang dieses Beitrags zum *American Way of Life* herbeiführten. Mit ihrem Wegfall entstand eine neue Kategorie des Kunstobjektes. Sie wurden zu einem begehrten neuen Sammlerobjekt sowie Bestandteil des kollektiven amerikanischen Gedächtnisses. Heute bietet dieses Thema einen faszinierenden Einblick in die amerikanischen Essgewohnheiten des 20. Jahrhunderts und erinnert auch – mit etwas Wehmut – an Zeiten, als das Leben noch einfacher war.

Cuisine kitsch

Durant presque tout le XXe siècle, la maîtresse de maison a été l'objet d'une attention soutenue de la part des publicitaires. Les tâches de la femme recluse au foyer sont nombreuses : éducation des enfants, ménage, repassage, courses, et surtout, préparation des repas pour toute la famille. La cuisine est son royaume et c'est dans la cuisine que Aunt Jemima®, Jell-O®, Weber® et Velveeta® rivalisent pour attirer son attention et obtenir sa fidélité à la marque.

Dès le tout début du siècle, les grandes entreprises alimentaires ont compris l'intérêt de distribuer aux ménagères des brochures présentant leurs produits et proposant des recettes qui les utilisent. Ces plaquettes, qui inondent le marché, obtiennent un tel succès qu'elles deviennent les accessoires obligés de toute cuisine. Presque toutes les entreprises qui fabriquent des ustensiles ou des appareils culinaires éditent ces brochures. Sardines, dattes, farine, fromage, bœuf, crème fouettée, riz, pommes de terre, tous les aliments sont accompagnés d'un opuscule chantant leurs louanges.

Les géants de l'industrie sont bientôt imités par les PME : boucheries industrielles, laiteries, producteurs d'œufs, d'agrumes ou encore le Comité de l'Avocat, éditent à leur tour des brochures vantant leurs produits respectifs et les meilleures façons de les accommoder. Elles sont distribuées gratuitement lors de foires commerciales ou à l'épicerie locale. Les fabricants d'électroménager eux aussi se rallient à cette technique commerciale et joignent des livres de recettes à leurs mixers, fours et autres barbecues. Ils sont imités par les fabricants de conserves ou de poêles qui voient dans cette littérature l'occasion rêvée de démontrer pourquoi leurs produits sont indispensables.

Mais c'est encore l'envoi postal qui demeure le meilleur moyen de toucher les ménagères. Un encart publicitaire dans un magazine permet de nouer un premier contact. L'heureuse maîtresse de maison qui envoie le coupon-réponse reçoit inévitablement une brochure par retour du courrier. Il arrive aussi que les livres de recettes soient insérés dans l'emballage ou attachés au produit lui-même.

Les images de ces plaquettes illustrent souvent avec brio l'ingéniosité de leur conception et c'est avant tout pour la qualité des illustrations que ces opuscules sont aujourd'hui recherchés par les collectionneurs. Si la plupart d'entre eux sont l'œuvre d'artistes et d'illustrateurs commerciaux anonymes, il existe quelques exceptions comme certaines plaquettes pour Jell-O® dues au talent de Maxfield Parrish. La première moitié du siècle abonde en artistes qui ont mis en scène avec brio des ingrédients et des ustensiles culinaires dans un graphisme très stylisé. Réalisées par des maîtres de la couleur et de la composition, ces illustrations devaient fasciner le public par leur représentation irrésistible des créations de l'art culinaire. La ménagère était souvent bien en peine de reproduire ces somptueuses interprétations artistiques, mais cet inconvénient n'ôtait rien à l'efficacité de leur impact visuel. Les premières tentatives de photographies culinaires sont moins probantes, mais les progrès de la technologie aidant, la photo finit par s'imposer dans la plupart des brochures de ce type à partir des années 1950.

La réduction progressive du temps consacré à la préparation de repas servis à heure fixe, peu à peu remplacés par des collations de type *fast-food*, signe la fin du règne des petits livres de recettes distribués gratuitement. Et la publicité télévisée engloutit l'essentiel des budgets des annonceurs, au détriment des magazines. En outre, les coûts additionnels d'impression et de diffusion des plaquettes finissent par avoir raison de cette vieille pratique commerciale typiquement américaine mais finalement peu rentable. Leur disparition a créé une nouvelle catégorie d'objets d'art et de mémoire américains et un champ d'exploration fertile pour les collectionneurs. Ces documents fournissent aussi un aperçu intéressant sur les habitudes alimentaires américaines au XXe siècle et constituent un aimable rappel d'une époque moins tourmentée que la nôtre.

24 Tempting RIPPLED WHEAT Recipes

"PHILLY" DIP

Party Handbook

500 *tasty*
SNACKS
IDEAS FOR ENTERTAINING

A *new* barbecue sandwich!

It's extra good with a cheese topping of America's finest slices

8 full ounce slices. Easy as peeling a banana!

GOOD HOUSEKEEPING'S

Egg and cheese Spaghetti and rice

DISHES

tempting, satisfying and flavor-filled

CHEESE
And ways to serve it

Price 10c

Good Things to Eat Made with Bread

John Dough
raised on
*Fleischmann's
Yeast*

The Fleischmann Co.

BRIGHT IDEAS
with
versatile
VELVEETA

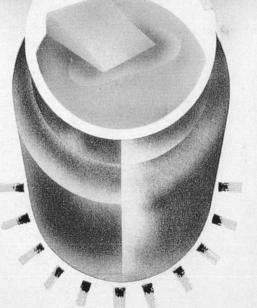

From the Kraft Kitchen

CHEESE

How Many
Do You Know
(See Below)

Zest AT ITS BEST !

Doesn't just looking at those delicious cheeses make you hungry?

Each kind has its own distinct flavor ... but every one has a tang and zest you can't find in any other food.

Zest at its *best*—because cheese contains the health-giving elements of milk, which is *nature's best in food!*

Serve cheese more often ... it's good for every member of the family!

Get acquainted with more varieties of cheese, starting with the seven kinds above: (1) Brick (2) Cottage (3) Cheddar (4) Camembert (5) Swiss (6) Bleu (7) in the middle, Edam! Actually, there are more than 400 *other* kinds of cheese, including Gorgonzola, Parmesan, Provolone ... a cheese to *every taste.*

They're all good ... and good *for* you!

AMERICAN DAIRY ASSOCIATION
20 N. Wacker Drive Building • Chicago 6, Illinois

This is Life

Standing Rib Roast of Prime Beef
—you may not find it every time you look for it in your store . . . but it's on its way back!

The protein of all meat (regardless of cut or kind) is complete. It contains all of the amino acids essential to life.

Children must have them for growth. Everyone, young and old, must have them to maintain tissues, regenerate blood, resist infections, rebuild the body after injury or illness.

This Seal means that all nutritional statements made in this advertisement are acceptable to the Council on Foods and Nutrition of the American Medical Association.

This is not just a piece of meat . . . this is something a man wants to come home to . . . something that helps children to grow . . . something that makes women proud of their meals.

This is a symbol of man's desire, his will to survive. For as old as man's instinct to live is his liking for meat. And to be satisfied in its eating.

Is it any wonder that, as meat moves back to the Home Plate, we look on meat with new regard, not just for its enjoyment, but as a nutritional cornerstone of life?

AMERICAN MEAT INSTITUTE · · · Headquarters, Chicago · · · Members throughout the U.S.

TIMELY MEAT RECIPES
FOR MEAL APPEAL

Morning

Noon

and Night

Compliments

NATIONAL LIVE STOCK
AND MEAT BOARD

My best MEAT Recipes

Compliments of

National Live Stock and Meat Board

SWIFT'S

FRAN

The Americ

BY

Martha Logan

SWIFT & COMPANY

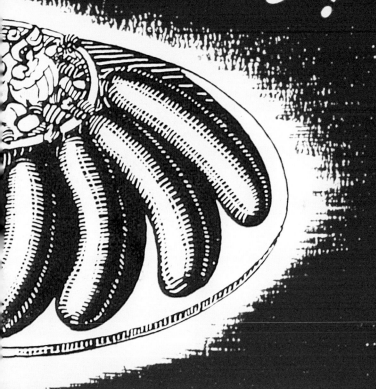

PREMIUM
FURTS

n Favorite !

HOME ECONOMIST
CHICAGO 9, ILLINOIS

250 *ways to prepare* MEAT

New ideas and old favorites...*plus* pages and pictures that show you exactly what to do to prepare the meat you buy for successful meals.

Make Every HAM a PERFECT ONE

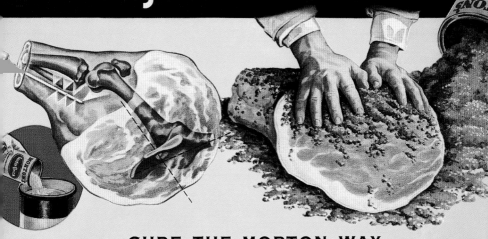

CURE THE MORTON WAY

FIRST — Mix Morton's Tender-Quick with water that has been boiled and cooled. Stir until dissolved. Then—with the meat pump, uniformly distribute this rich Tender-Quick curing pickle along the bones. This immediately starts the cure right next to the bone, offsetting the chance of taint and giving a uniform cure in the center of the meat.

NEXT — Rub Morton's Sugar-Cure over the entire outside surface of the meat. This nationally known and specially prepared sugar-curing salt, with its appetizing, rich, smoke flavor and balanced spices, strikes in from the outside, curing toward the bone area. You get a finer, richer flavor with no under-cured spots in any part of the meat.

Richness, Beautiful Color, Wonderful Flavor

Hams that make that rich, red gravy — that are tender and juicy . . . hams that are as sweet as a nut right down to the bone. That's what you want! Hams that your whole family will enjoy . . . the kind that your neighbors will envy. And, hams that are so thoroughly cured that even the bone and the last shred of meat can be used to make that wonderful "second-helping" bean soup.

There are many reasons why a million farmers last year cured the Morton Way . . . and why farm publications, county agents and farm leaders recommend this way of perfect curing. They know that as soon as the butchering is done, the "battle at the ham bone" starts . . . that meat curing is a race between the curing action of the salt and the forces that are working against you to make for lower quality. They know that pumping along the bone with Tender-Quick to start the cure from the inside — and then curing from the outside with Morton's Sugar-Cure — means a thorough, uniform, even cure. A ham with no under-cured or over-cured spots . . . no spoilage of meat—no bone taint.

It's so easy—so simple—to make every ham a perfect one. After all, it is the cure itself that is the secret of making fine hams and bacon. Everything necessary for a perfect cure is contained in Morton's Sugar-Cure and Tender-Quick. The salt, the fast, super quality curing ingredients, the pure maple and cane sugars, the rare spices and rich, smoke flavor . . . all properly blended and all working together . . . give you meat with a flavor and texture that cannot be obtained by any other curing method. It is impossible to home-mix the salt and other curing ingredients equal to Morton's Sugar-Cure and Tender-Quick.

Without question, this is *the* year to cure your meat better than it has ever been cured before. The meat you will eat is worth much more in dollars and cents. Don't be satisfied with an ordinary cure. Don't try to save a few cents on the cure and sacrifice dollars in quality.

Cure the Morton Way! More than eight million hams were cured last year, as pictured above. This year—additional millions will be cured. Also shoulders, bacon, loins, etc. . . . In ever-increasing numbers, farm families are turning to the Morton Way of meat curing . . . these families are actually making every ham a perfect one.

HOME MEAT CURING *made easy*

GET YOUR COPY NOW!
See Your Dealer — Only 10c
Here is a complete, illustrated guide to meat curing. More than 100 pages of pictures, charts, diagrams and simple, clear directions covering pork, beef, lamb, sausage, poultry and smoked turkey. Your local merchant has these books for sale — ask him — only 10¢ a copy.

MORTON'S Sugar-Cure FOR HAMS & BACON *Cures Fast* Imparts Rich Smoke Flavor

MORTON'S Tender-Quick

MORTON'S

DELICIOUS SAUSAGE
Morton's Sausage Seasoning is ready to use, perfectly proportioned and blended, including salt and all necessary ingredients. You'll make sausage that hits the spot every time—sausage with just the right amount of zest and flavor. A 10-ounce can seasons 30 pounds of sausage.

MORTON SALT COMPANY, CHICAGO

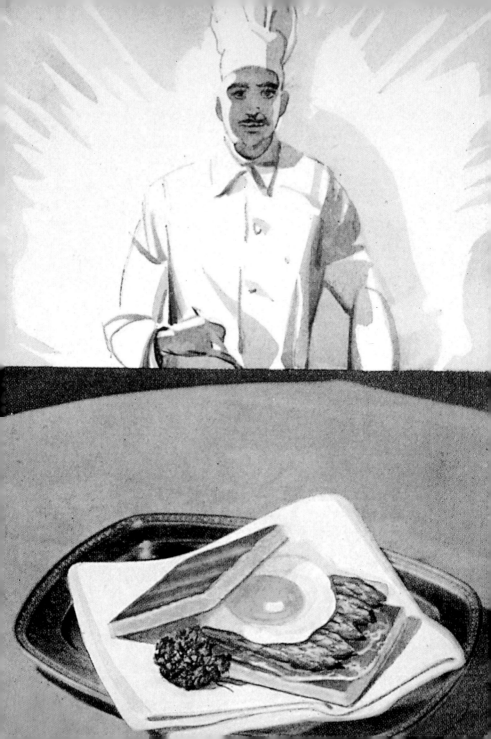

THE BEST FROM THE WEST WITH HONEY

HOW TO *freeze* MEAT, POULTRY, FISH, FRUIT AND VEGETABLES

WITH
GOOD LUCK
THE ORIGINAL COLD PACK
RUBBERS

All out for a

Chick-n-Que

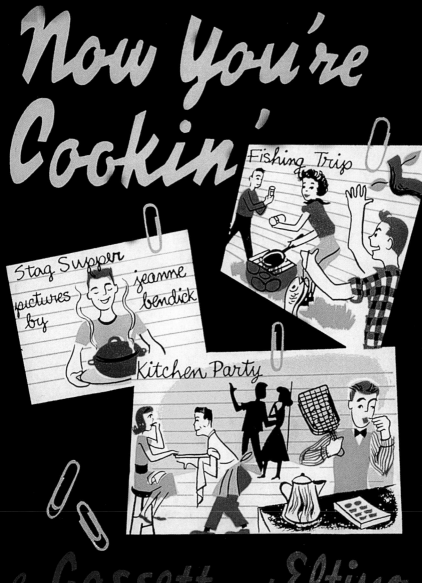

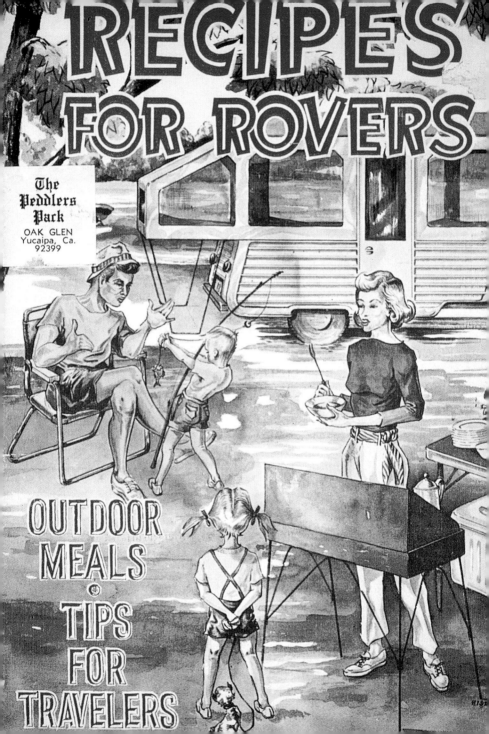

RECIPES FOR ROVERS

OUTDOOR MEALS
TIPS FOR TRAVELERS

metropolitan
COOK
BOOK

KNOX

Salad Book

—with a Special Section
on Molded Salads

THE
New
FRUIT
FOR
SMART
SALADS

CALAVO
The Aristocrat of Salad Fruits

The MAZOLA *Salad Bowl*

BANANA *Salad Bazaar*

the salad bowl

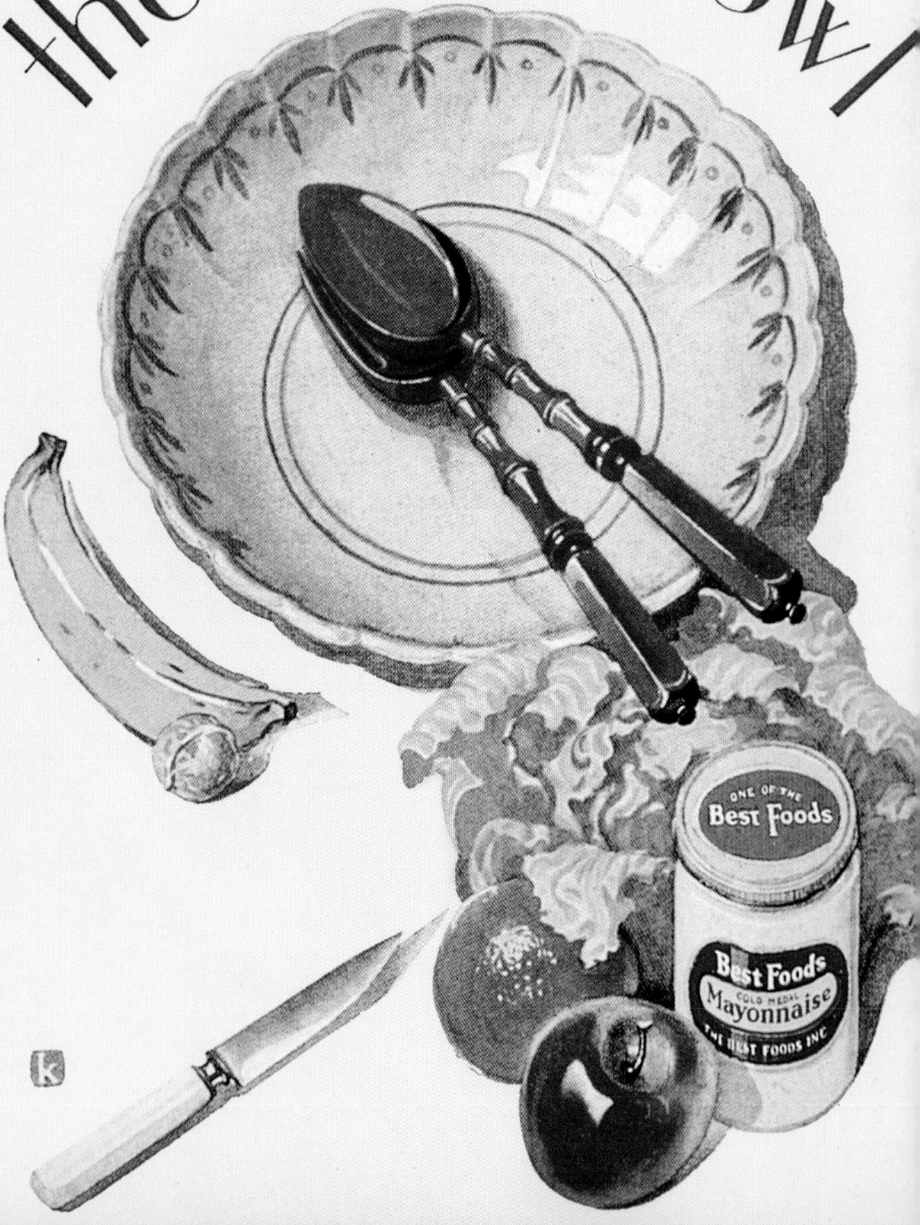

Salad Dressings

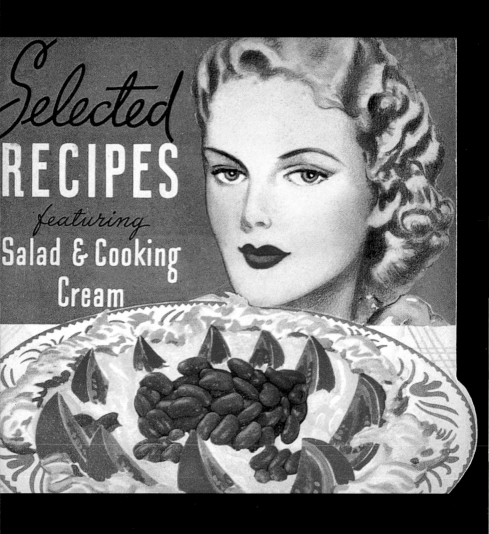

Selected
RECIPES
featuring
Salad & Cooking
Cream

CHICKEN PACIFIC

CAPTIVATING CATSU
and PICKLE RECIPES

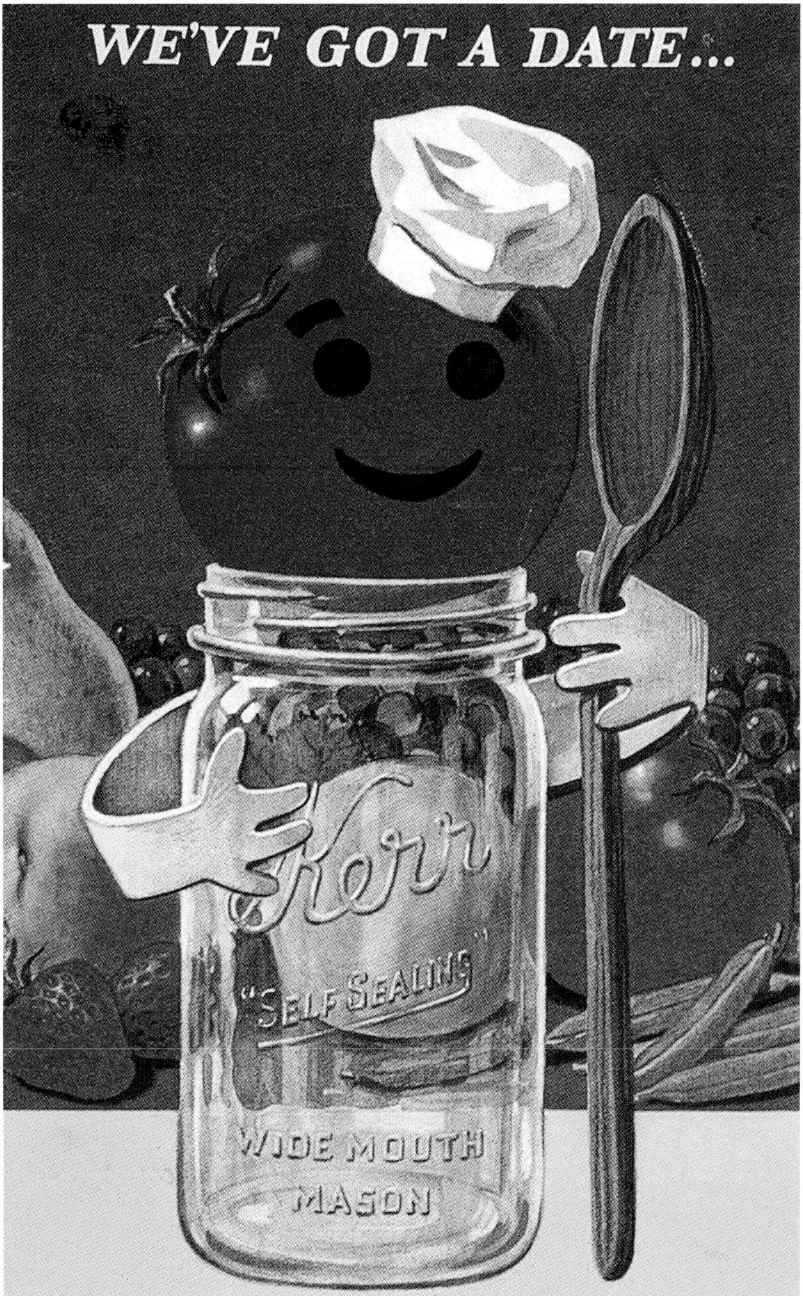
WE'VE GOT A DATE...
Kerr
"SELF SEALING"
WIDE MOUTH
MASON

HAWAIIAN
PINEAPPLE

SLICED --- CRUSHED

Now for **FRESH STRAWBERRIES**

TRY THESE DELICIOUS WAYS TO SERVE THEM

Suggested by

E·A·Morrison INC. GROCER

SUNKIST ORANGE RECIPES

for Year-round Freshness!

Sunkist
RECIPES
for Every Day

Jell-O
Fruit
Cocktail

What Mrs. Dewey did with the NEW JELL-O!

Enjoy them
ALL YEAR 'ROUND

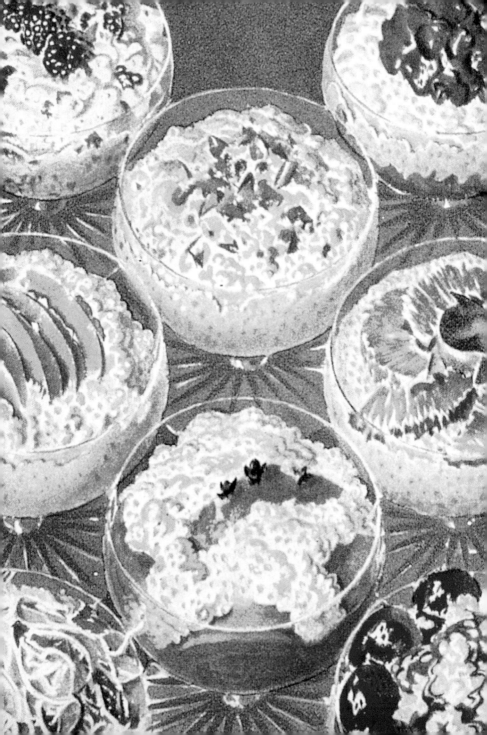

1

2

4

THE KING AND QUEEN MIGHT EAT THEREOF
AND NOBLEMEN BESIDES

JELL-O
Book of Menus

FOOD FASHIONS OF THE HOUR

SPRING · SUMMER · AUTUMN · WINTER

Joys of JELL-O

BRAND

GELATIN DESSERT

Bright Spots

FOR
WARTIME MEALS

66 RATION-WISE RECIPES

ROYAL
FRUIT
GELATIN
SUGGESTIONS

Made by the Makers of ROYAL BAKING POWDER

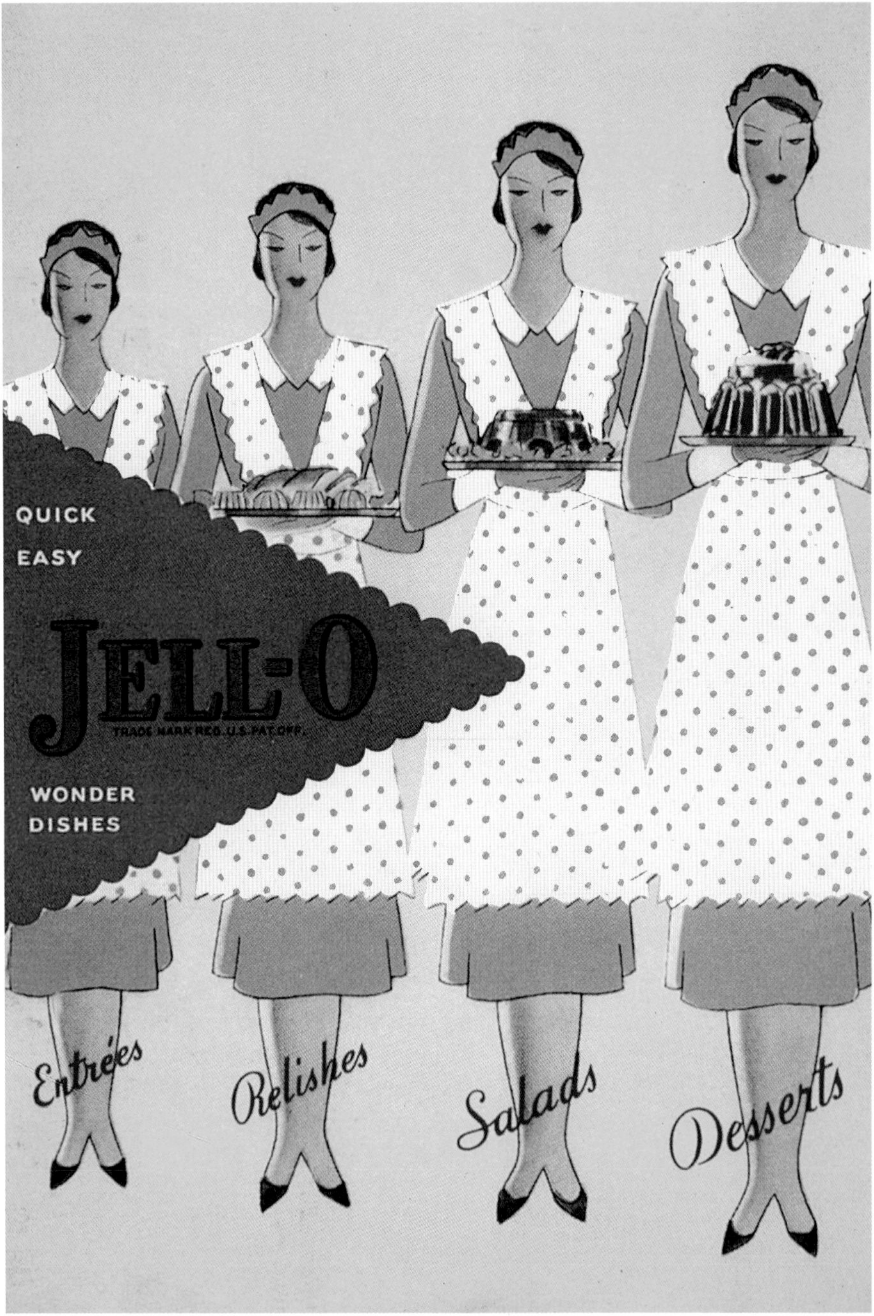
QUICK
EASY
JELL-O
TRADE MARK REG. U.S. PAT. OFF.
WONDER
DISHES
Entrées
Relishes
Salads
Desserts

Prize *dairy dishes*

'NO-SIFT' RECIPES
DEVELOPED
ESPECIALLY FOR
ROBIN HOOD
PRE-SIFTED FLOUR

Let's Bake

THE ROBIN HOOD 'NO-SIFT' WAY

The Prince of the Gelatin Isles

Newest Member of the Post Cereal Family
POST ALPHA-BITS

A nourishing, new oat cereal your whole family will love

Here's a healthful, crisp oat cereal that literally spells delicious goodness. Gives you high-quality cereal protein with just the right amount of sugar. Helps provide the quick energy and body-building nourishment everyone needs. No wonder Post Alpha-Bits is the cereal mothers love to serve and children love to eat.

Nourishing Goodness *from* A *to* Z

 Post —THE CEREALS THAT HAPPEN TO BE "JUST A LITTLE BIT BETTE

NEW OAT CEREAL

Post

ALPHA-BITS

SUGAR SPARKLED ABC's

COOK BOOK

A PICTURE COOK BOOK FOR CHILDREN

FOR BOYS AND GIRLS 7-12

BIB 'n' TUCKERS

Most gracious still, for those who care,
Is dinner with a formal air.

Christmas Tree Flip Cake

3 tbsp. butter	8 pecan halves
½ cup brown sugar (packed)	1½ cups BISQUICK
1 can (8 oz.) small pineapple slices (reserve juice)	¾ cup sugar
	3 tbsp. soft shortening
1 maraschino cherry, cut into 8 slices	1 egg
	¾ cup milk
	1 tsp. vanilla

Heat oven to 350° (mod.). Melt butter over low heat in layer pan, 9x1½". Mix in brown sugar; spread over bottom. Arrange fruit and nuts (directions below). Make batter by combining Bisquick, sugar, shortening, egg and ⅓ cup of milk. Beat vigorously 1 min. Gradually stir in remaining milk and vanilla. Beat ½ min. Pour batter over fruit in pan. Bake 40 to 45 min., until toothpick stuck into center comes out clean. Invert at once on serving plate. Allow pan to remain over cake for a couple minutes so sugar mixture will run down over cake. Serve warm—plain or with whipped cream.

To decorate: Add ½ tsp. green food coloring to pineapple juice. Cut each of 3 pineapple slices into eighths. Put half of pieces into green juice for minute or two. Drain both pineapple and cherry slices well on absorbent paper. Place nuts at even intervals around edge of pan to form stems. To form trees, make a triangle of 5 pineapple pieces. Alternate a green and yellow tree (4 trees of each). Place cherry slices at top of each tree.

Tapper Suppers!

Gay buffets are winning ways to celebrate the holidays.

16

Betty Crocker's MERRY MAKINGS

Fun Foods for Happy Entertaining

Royal Gelatins and Puddings

171 Recipes

TAPIOCA PUDDINGS

ROYAL
RECIPE
PARADE

Peter Pan PEANUT BUTTER
in your Daily Diet

WAKE UP
to Aunt Jemima Pancakes!

So <u>light</u>-So <u>tender</u>
they melt in your mouth!

No Wonder...
more women prefer Aunt Jemima
than all other brands <u>combined</u>!

Let your fork sink into the fluffy lightness of a stack of golden Aunt
Jemima Pancakes. Ever see such fine, fluffy texture? Ever taste such
melting tenderness? Now you know why homemakers everywhere
choose these better pancakes. Treat your folks to America's favorites
tomorrow morning!

AUNT JEMIMA
Pancakes and Waffles

Design for Living
...Graciously

WITH A NEW
ROPER
GAS RANGE

ALLTROL "CENTER-SIMMER" TOP BURNERS ARE MUCH FASTER...MORE EFFICIENT ...IDEAL EVERY WAY

"BAKE-MASTER" OVENS PRE-HEAT FASTER... BAKE AND ROAST WHILE USING LESS FUEL

"ROPER-GLO" BROILER BURNERS BROIL BIG, THICK STEAK IN 10 MINUTES OR LESS

built to "CP" standards

"AMERICA'S FINEST"...PERFORMANCE PROVES IT!

The great new ROPER automatic gas ranges provide a carefree cooking service that's superior in every respect. Utilizing Gas, the nation's favorite fuel, they assure the ultimate in speed, cleanliness, convenience and economy. More than 69 years of gas range manufacturing experience has contributed to the host of exclusive ROPER features you can enjoy today. Choose *your* new ROPER from the most complete line of gas ranges in the industry. Write for Free Folder T. Ask your ROPER retailer about these new beauties. Geo. D. Roper Corporation, Rockford, Illinois.

- **ROPER GAS RANGES • ROPER GAS RANGES IN DECORATOR COLORS**
- **ROPER "arRANGEable" BUILT-IN GAS COOKING UNITS**
- **ROPER "DRY-AIRE" GAS CLOTHES DRYERS**

GAS

INDUSTRIAL · COMMERCIAL · RESIDENTIAL

AUTHENTIC CHINESE RECIPES

MIN SUN TRADING CO.

Importers and Manufacturers of

CHINESE MAID PRODUCTS

2222 S. LaSalle Street, Chicago 16, Illinois

飲食衣著勿忘戒律

Chinese Magic

with Leftovers

easy EVERBEST ways
to turn icebox
oddments into
delicious Chinese dishes

Miss Fluffy's

RICE
COOK BOOK

Miss Fluffy Rice

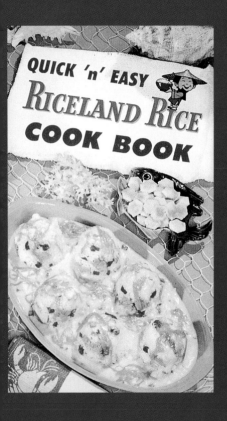

QUICK 'n' EASY
RICELAND RICE
COOK BOOK

WATER
MAID

WHITE
UNCOATED
RICE

Quality Supreme

2 POUNDS   NET WEIGHT

DR CALDWELL'S

GUIDE TO
HEALTH

HOME COOK
BOOK

PUBLISHED BY

PEPSIN SYRUP COMPANY

MONTICELLO   ILLINOIS

BEST FOR EVERY PURPOSE
WASHBURN CROSBY'S
GOLD MEDAL FLOUR
Eventually WHY NOT NOW?

Sixty-five Delicious Dishes

Made
with
Bread

THE FLEISCHMANN CO.
Fleischmann's Yeast

RECIPES

GEISHA
BRAND
CRAB
IT HAS NO EQUALS

Fleischmann's Recipes

55 Ways to Save Eggs

ROYAL BAKING POWDER CO.,
NEW YORK, U.S.A.

Making
BISCUITS

Some Sunday Night Menus

OW TO MAKE BISCUITS - *the Day Before!* - SUCCESSFUL
SCUIT MAKING — DELICIOUS RECIPES FOR BISCUITS
MUFFINS AND QUICK BREADS

Home Baking Made Easy
FOR BEGINNERS AND EXPERTS

Weber's
LUNCH BOX MENUS

RECIPES FOR
Sandwiches
AND OTHER APPETIZING
WAYS of SERVING
Bread

Compliments of
REGAN BRO.'S CO.
whose MINNEAPOLIS bread
is sold all over the
North-West

Ask for "Regan's" when you buy bread
PLEASE SEE BACK COVER

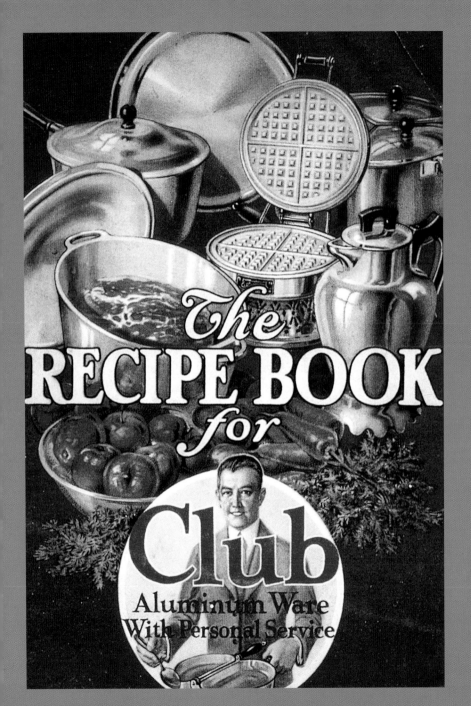

The RECIPE BOOK for

Club

Aluminum Ware
With Personal Service

CHOICE RECIPES

REG. U.S.
PAT. OFF.

COMPLIMENTS OF
WALTER BAKER & CO., LTD
DORCHESTER, MASS.
ESTABLISHED 1780.

SOUR CREAM
The Gourmet Touch
to Everyday Cooking

SOUR
CREAM

...make mine with

Marshmallows!

MARCIA CAMP'S MODERN RECIPES

NEW

PARTY ♥ CAKES

FOR ALL OCCASIONS

Rainbow Sandwich Loaf, page 7

RAINBOW COLOR-SCHEME

RAINBOW color-schemes are especially beautiful for bridal or engagement showers, summer birthday parties, summer porch or card parties, lawn parties, etc.

Rainbow Cookies page 7

FEATHER CAKE WITH PINEAPPLE FROSTING
(Recipe pages 18 and 24)

...RY SHORTCAKE
...ges 10 and 30)

Cake Secrets

American Beauty
Cake
page 15

ROSE OR

PINK

COLOR-

SCHEME

Christmas Tree
Cake
page 24

Bridge Party
Cake
page 20

Bunco Layer Cake
page 20

Circus
Birthday Cake
page 29

Clowns, page 29

Edible Place Cards
page 3

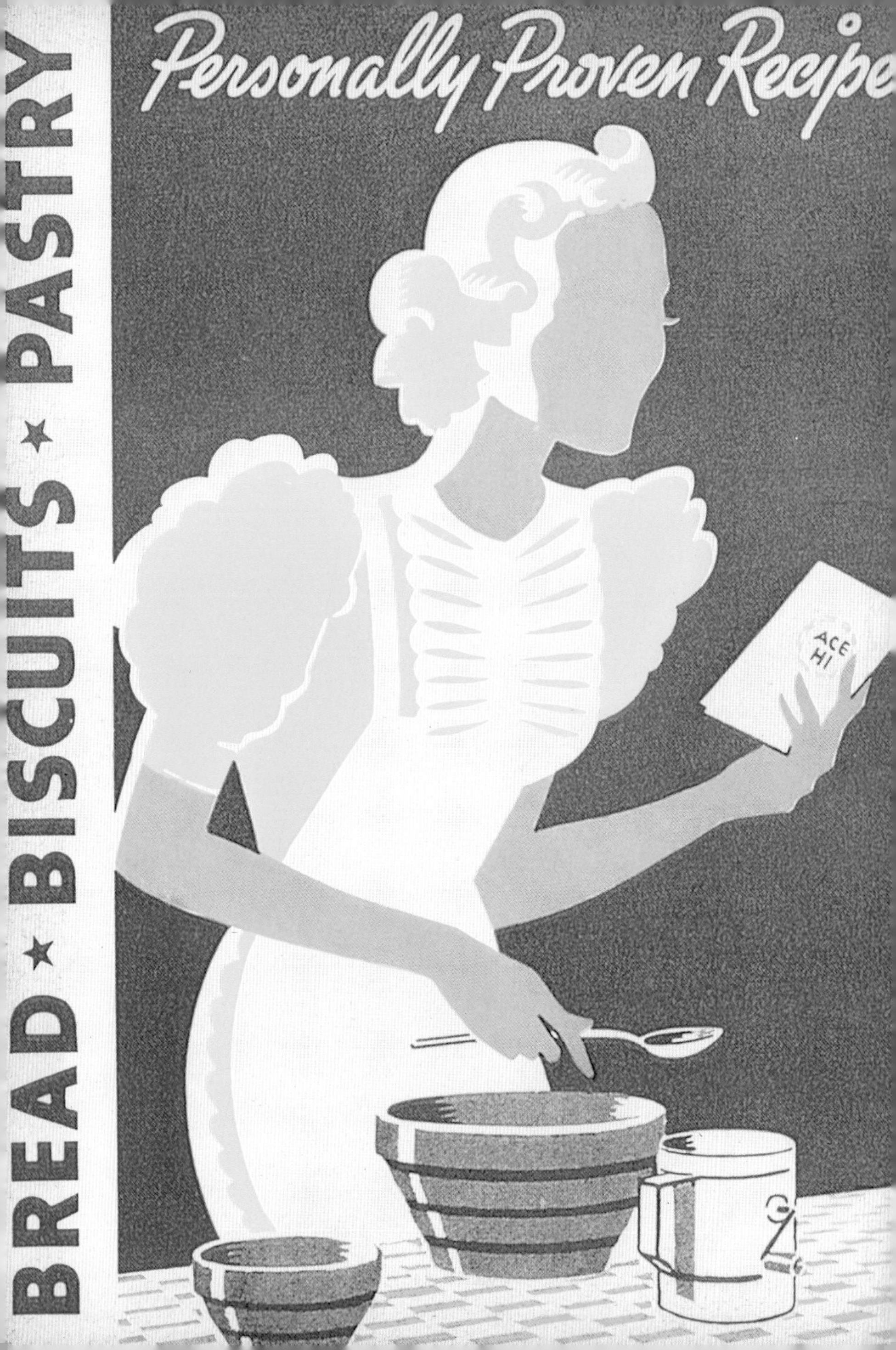
Personally Proven Recipe
BREAD ★ BISCUITS ★ PASTRY
ACE HI

GOOD LUCK
MARGARINE
RECIPES

FROZEN
Salads and Desserts

by Mary Blake

SUNKIST
Fresh Grapefruit
RECIPES

Frigidaire
Frozen Delights

Volume

1

French Specialties

Harwood & Tjaden's

Wonderful World of Cooking

by

Ruth Conrad Bateman

author of
"I Love to Cook Book"

MAKE AGAIN RECIPES INSPIRED BY CANNED PINEAPPLE

HAWAII

THE ALOHA STATE

NEW YORK WORLD'S FAIR
1964-1965
SOUVENIR RECIPES

FOODS from SUNNY LANDS

Keep on the Sunny Side of Life

A new way of living

New Uses for Catsup
CALIFORNIA HOME BRAND
TOMATO CATSUP
CALIFORNIA CONSERVING COMPANY, Inc.

HOW TO DUNK

For Children, Adults
and Octogenarians

Official Handbook

HILLS ❦ BROS
COFFEE

Red Can Brand   *The Original Vacuum Pack*

®

"Mom always says —
any cereal assortment ... as long as it's
Post-Tens!"

DICK SARGENT

MOTHER'S BIGGEST LITTLE HELPER is Post-Tens. Lets you choose just the cereal you want—when you want it. Roasted, toasted, popped or puffed . . . seven delicious cereals, fresh as morning. We say *anybody* can please *everybody*—with Post-Tens.

"ALL POST CEREALS HAPPEN TO BE JUST A LITTLE BIT BETTER"

FRESH! POST-TENS CRISP!

The Breakfast Foods of General Foods

Any corn flakes are <u>real gone</u>...
as long as they're Post Toasties

REAL GONE—THAT'S FOR SURE...both the miss and her corn flakes! They're Post Toasties—rolled and toasted a special way that keeps the sweet corn flavor in each curly bit o' crispness. No wonder folks call them the "little bit better" corn flakes. Go ahead—taste 'em yourself!

The Breakfast Foods of General Foods

"ALL POST CEREALS HAPPEN TO BE JUST A LITTLE BIT BETTER"

THE STORY of SHRIMP

NATIONAL SHRIMP CANNERS ASSOCIATION
HIBERNIA BANK BUILDING
NEW ORLEANS, LA.

serve a 7-UP punch
...put a
SURPRISE
in your
party!

GUASTI
BRAND
PRODUCTS
PRODUCED BY
ITALIAN
VINEYARD CO.
LOS ANGELES

Acknowledgements

Special thanks to Cindy Vance for her unabashed enthusiasm in digitally producing and designing the book. The unaccounted hours of service above-and-beyond the call of duty is deeply appreciated.

Additional thanks go out to all the image merchants whose uncanny ability to find and provide me with many of the gems included in this book. They are the true keepers of history and I am grateful for their generosity, friendship and advice.

All images are from the Martha Spelman collection. Inquiries concerning the collection can be directed to art@marthaproductions.com. Aunt Jemima® is a registered trademark of The Quaker Oats Company. Weber® is a registered trademark of Weber-Stephen Products Co. Velveeta® and Jell-O® are registered trademarks of KF Holdings. Any omissions for credit or copyright are un-intentional and appropriate credit will be given in future editions if such copyright holders contact the publisher.

© 2002 TASCHEN GmbH
Hohenzollernring 53, D–50672 Köln
www.taschen.com

Art Direction & Design: Jim Heimann, L. A.
Digital Composition & Design: Cindy Vance, Modern Art & Design, L. A.
Cover Design: Claudia Frey, Cologne
Production: Tina Ciborowius, Cologne
Editorial coordination: Sonja Altmeppen, Cologne
German translation: Gabriele Gugetzer, Hamburg
French translation: Daniel Roche, Paris

Printed in Italy
ISBN 3–8228–1496–2

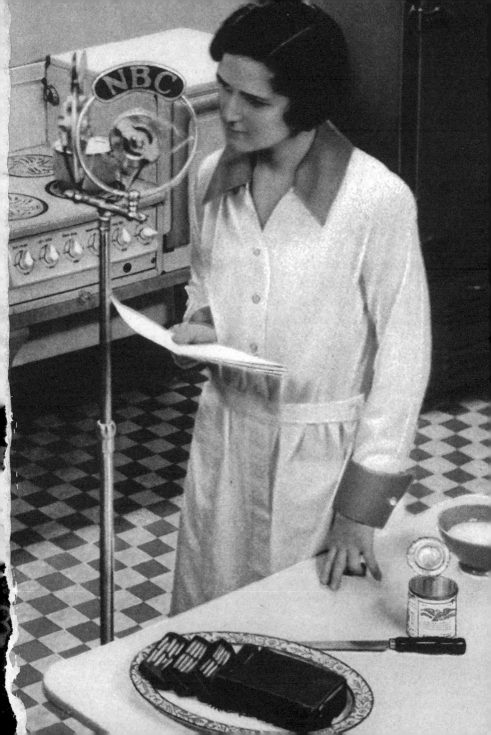